GOLD NUGGETS and SILVER BULLETS

John Grogan

Evergreen PRESS

Gold Nuggets and Silver Bullets
by John Grogan

ISBN 1-58169-113-0
For Worldwide Distribution
Printed in the U.S.A.

Evergreen Press
P.O. Box 191540 • Mobile, AL 36619
800-367-8203

Table of Contents

Section I—Gold Nuggets for Your Life

Section II—Silver Bullets for Your Career

DEDICATION

This book is dedicated to you,
the reader, for your interest in exploring
new perspectives.

INTRODUCTION

From time to time we encounter ideas, facts, or situations that challenge our perceptions. Because they might be inconsistent with our cherished beliefs, we either defend those beliefs by discounting the new information, or we accept them. The most enlightening message in the world cannot exceed the self-image of the person hearing it.

This is a book of light and salt. It will, hopefully, illuminate some area of life or perhaps give you a fresh perspective, while flavoring your life with the saltiness of truth.

GOLD NUGGETS

...for Your Life

1

The Enemy of Fear

Fear knocked at the door, and hope opened it to find no one there. How do *you* open the doors of opportunity in life—with fear or with hope?

I can remember sitting in pitch darkness in a seminar once when the moderator asked us if we could hear the darkness resist as he turned the lights back on in the room. He went through this exercise several times, but no one ever heard the darkness resist as it fled. With illumination, the darkness of ignorance and fear must flee. It has no choice!

Fear causes inertia and "makes us lose the good we oft might win," Shakespeare said. One of the greatest fears is that of the unknown, which causes us to miss all the abundance that God has for us. I have a friend who has a son in college. Recently I asked him what his boy was going to be when he gets out of school. He thought for a moment and then said, "Forty-two, I think!" "Some people are always getting ready to live," Emerson said, "but never living."

Obviously, some fear is normal in keeping us out of harm's way, but it should never paralyze us. We are born with very few fears. Most of them we have learned along the way.

The real tragedy of fear is its self-fulfilling prophecy—what we fear will come upon us if we focus upon it. We experience failure because we are overwhelmed by our fear. We need to realize that if we steadfastly hold onto our hope, the dragons of fear and doubt will disappear and we can experience victory.

Heroism in the midst of great peril results from overcoming our fears. While failure looks back and fear looks around, hope looks ahead. The enemy of fear is hope!

May integrity and uprightness protect me, because my hope is in you (Psalm 25:21).

Be strong and take heart, all you who hope in the LORD (Psalm 231:24).

2

THE PINNED-DOWN PERSON

In fictitious Camelot, King Arthur cries out, "If I am to die in battle, please, please, don't let me die bewildered." Many of us today stand bewildered over why we do the things we don't want to do and fail to do the things we ought to do. The Apostle Paul struggled with this same difficult, complex, and bewildering dilemma in Romans 7:18:

> *I know that nothing good lives in me, that is, in my sinful nature. For I have the desire to do what is good, but I cannot carry it out.*

Make no miscalculation—the chief delight of the devil is the defeat of man through his own weakness. He cannot defeat God, but he can defeat what God has created.

Really, there are just three ways in which we can begin to change our situation:

1) We become motivated. Motivation appeals to the emotions, but unfortunately, this emotion is short lived. Emotions will not sustain a vision. (Prov. 29:18, Judges 17:6). This is one reason why, for example, New Year's resolutions fail.

2) We change due to an appeal to our intellect. Through insight, or additional information, we take an action that results in permanent improvement: we change our eating habits, we begin using our seat belt, we join AA, or we take steps to stop smoking.

3) We change because our present behavior is generating so much pain and discomfort that we are left with zero options. At this point in one's life it's either change or suicide. And suicide does not always mean a physical death; it can be a walking, living death. I believe that when most people come to this point, they let God do business with them because of their weariness and exhaustion. Just because we are at the end of our rope does not mean that we are at the end of our hope.

In Second Corinthians 5:17, Paul says, "Therefore if any man be in Christ, he is a new creature; old things are passed away; behold, all things are become new." A new "divine nature," which comes only through Jesus Christ, is our only hope for breaking the bonds that hold us (Rom. 8:13-14). In things eternal, God is the genuine article.

3

PAYING THE PRICE FOR CHANGE

A rut is a grave with both ends kicked out. The reason many people settle for a rut is because they get kicked in the head every time they attempt to climb out.

Don't be surprised or discouraged over the lack of support you receive when you resolve to change your life. The greatest resistance will always come from those closest to you because most people generally think in critical, judgmental terms rather than in positive, creative ones. And those who know you best remember your past shortfalls and failures.

The people we look to most for support will generally have one of three reactions, and perhaps all three in sequence. The first will be one of disbelief: "You're going to do what?" The second reaction will be an attempt to save us from ourselves because they are thinking we've gone off our rails. The third reaction will be detailed criticism, and there aren't many of us who can stand up under it. If we are committed to change, we must be prepared to stand alone.

Success has a thousand fathers while failure is an orphan. When we become successful, we hear comments like: "I knew he could do it!" or, "I always knew she had the right stuff!" But if we fail in the slightest way, we have people ready to point the finger at us and say, "I told you so!"

In truth, the average mind produces opinionated criticism that hinders, rather than creative ideas that help. An opinion is the cheapest thing in the world. To rain on someone else's parade by offering unsolicited opinions or judgmental pronouncements is to play God. Unless there's a risk of catastrophic financial loss or physical, mental, emotional, or spiritual damage, let people make their own mistakes. We learn best through attempting to accomplish something.

While it is true that there is safety and wisdom in a number of counselors, there are times when we need to go our own way in order to break out of the rut and find the path God has destined for us to trod.

4

STANDING STRONG AND STEADY

Like a tree with deep roots, our ability to withstand the winds of adversity depends on our anchor. Can we flex without breaking?

A high wind will push over an oak tree and snap off a pine tree six to ten feet from the ground. But the palm tree will bend and bow but not break. Why? Because the palm tree has a taproot that goes deep into the ground and firmly anchors it.

Are you an oak tree? Do you keep getting knocked over by the high winds of life? If you are, remember that you don't have to remain there. I like the story about the fighter being interviewed by a reporter who asked, "What kind of fighter are you?" The fighter replied, "When I get knocked down, in my mind I'm getting right back up!" It's hard for life to beat a person like that.

Are you a pine tree? Pine trees take so much of

life's pressures and then one day they just snap, sometimes with cataclysmic consequences. Learn to bend and let the winds of trouble blow over you and not damage your core.

If you're a palm tree, you may ache and groan as you bend under the pressures of life, but you are not pushed over or broken. When the winds are gone, you will be able to stand straight once again.

We can make the transition from being an oak or a pine tree to a palm tree as long as we turn to the One who can help us.

I've heard it said that our character is forged in the midst of the test. We are revealed by the tests of life and remade from day to day as we attempt to pass each test that comes our way. Failure to prepare ourselves for the time of testing is like an army waiting until the battle to prepare its ordnance. Before the soldiers are ready to engage the enemy, they're wiped out! However, with preparation comes resilience.

5

THE FOUR TONGUES THAT WAG

What we say probably affects more people than any other action we take. Of the four tongues that wag, two should be emulated and two should be avoided.

The first speech pattern is the *disciplined or controlled tongue.* People with this pattern do something rare today: They think before they speak. Most of us speak when we feel like saying something, but the person with a controlled tongue speaks only when they have something constructive to say and so they are entrusted with other people's confidences.

The *concerned tongue* is the speech pattern of those who speak truthfully while seeking to encourage. Those with a caring tongue know that honest counsel, tempered by grace, is truth that sets them free. Sometimes truth hurts, but you have no friend or ally in someone who doesn't speak the truth to you. It's better to receive wounds from a friend than kisses from an enemy!

The *scheming tongue* is the speech of those who twist the truth. These people use cajolery and sweet talk to manipulate. Beware of flattering lips or a boastful tongue because deception is close at hand. In the end, people appreciate frankness more than flattery. People with scheming or conniving tongues deal in gossip and slander out of wrong motives.

The fourth tongue is the *careless or irresponsible tongue*. These people shoot from the lip. Trusting a person with this speech pattern is like running a race on a broken foot. "O many a shaft at random sent," Sir Walter Scott said, "finds marks the archer little meant." These people wound indiscriminately. They traffic in deception, half-truths, cutting remarks, and profanity. They are usually cynical and ruled by their emotions. Some would refer to these people as loose cannons.

Keep your tongue from evil and your lips from speaking lies (Ps. 34:13).

The tongue has the power of life and death (Pr. 18:21).

He who guards his mouth and his tongue keeps himself from calamity (Pr. 21:23).

6

THE HEALING BALM OF LAUGHTER

A notable sage once said, "I am suspicious of two kinds of people: those who fail to write things down and those who never laugh." While cerebral people can be contemplative to the point of seeming somber, there is something even more suspicious about someone who never laughs.

Laughter is a catharsis, a healing balm to our central nervous system. Some contend that it transforms the state of one's health. The late Norman Cousins, past editor of *Saturday Review* magazine, found this to be true when, at the peak of his career, he was undone by a withering illness. His doctors were totally perplexed by his condition and told him they held out little hope. Taking matters into his own hands, he had one of his aides bring him movies featuring the funniest slapstick comedians of the day. Norm Cousins literally laughed his way back to good health and was able to join the ranks of the productive for many long years afterwards.

There is something wholesome and energizing about a good belly laugh—a laughter that comes from the soul. I have a friend who reminds me of a Masai warrior because he's tall and noble in bearing. His laugh sounds like gentle thunder.

Laughter can express joy in a way nothing else can. The most restorative laughter is the beneficial kind that radiates from a soul that is well and rejoices in God's precious gift of life to us. We need more people around us with that kind of laughter.

> *And Sarah said, "God has made me laugh, and all who hear will laugh with me"* (Gen. 21:6).

> *He will yet fill your mouth with laughing, And your lips with rejoicing* (Job 8:21).

7

THE VALUE IN DELAY

All around us we see the sad results of people demanding, "I WANT IT ALL!" We are the richest and, I suspect, the most acquisitive nation ever known to mankind. Many of us go through life saying, "I want…" "I want…" "I want!"

The prudent among us have a grip on their impulses and rule over their appetites rather than being subject to them. They understand about their limitations and know that it's often easier to do a thing than to undo it. It's easier, for example, to spend money than to pay it back! And some of us have found that it's easier to form a corporation than to dissolve one; to rent than to evict; to hire than to fire; to say, "I do" rather than, "I don't want to anymore." Every one of our actions have consequences.

Wise people pause and think before they decide to plunge ahead. Impetuosity can create mean masters. An old proverb says, the rich rule over the poor and the borrower is servant to the lender. Will the people who are pawing at your purse strings be there for you when it's empty?

A friend of mine, who says the truly important things in life are rarely urgent, understands that delay can promote serenity. "Do we need to satisfy *all* our appetites?" he asks. How much is enough? Are we willing to enmesh ourselves in financial, legal, and emotional bondages to the point where we're afraid to answer the phone or retrieve our mail?

My friend has a theory about garage sales. He contends that the same stuff just keeps making the rounds of those who partake in them. Nobody needs any of it—they just like to acquire stuff.

A satisfied soul loathes the honeycomb, But to a hungry soul every bitter thing is sweet (Prov. 27:7).

All the labor of man is for his mouth, And yet the soul is not satisfied (Ec. 6:7).

8

WHERE HAVE ALL THE HEROES GONE?

The contemporary song, "Looking for Love in All the Wrong Places," describes how we search for our heroes. For example, there's an actor who was held in higher esteem by the youth of his era than most of their own fathers. Yet this celluloid man of true grit admitted that, in truth, he was afraid of women. He eventually died an unpleasant death from years of having smoked up to eight packs of cigarettes a day. His name was John Wayne.

Another man once changed a major segment of the entertainment world. So tall does he still stand in the Pantheon of our icons, that marriages are performed in his name. Fifty- and sixty-year-old women make yearly pilgrimages to the gift shop on his burial grounds to gather up yet more memorabilia. Many people have built shrines in their homes honoring this "king" who died over two decades ago. His name, of course, is Elvis Presley.

Another example of hero fever is ascribed to our sometimes vastly overpaid athletes. We can't seem to get enough of watching people bat a ball, drive a ball, kick a ball, throw a ball, roll a ball, or bounce a ball. As we learn from time to time, many of these players are little boys in men's bodies. They are victims of too much of a good thing and let their notoriety go to their hand by ignoring the rules the rest of us struggle to live by.

The real heroes are far removed from the theatrical limelight. They are the researchers working quietly, but diligently, on cures for the diseases that afflict us. They are parents trying to raise the next generation of responsible citizens. They are dedicated teachers, pastors, and civil servants. They are judges who refuse to say that the guilty are innocent, and the innocent are guilty. They are law enforcement officers who daily try to stem the tide of moral decay.

There are real heroes all around us if we take the time to look.

9

Death by Comparison

When actors and actresses are starting out, they quite often imitate the reigning idols of the time. This is all part of maturing, but failure to establish their own identity just about ensures them a short career. Continually comparing ourselves to others leads to insufferable arrogance or consuming despair. If people don't like us for who we are, they surely won't like us for who we aren't! Respect all men but deify none. We are all unique and created with our own special genetic promise.

If we're ever going to amount to a hill of beans, we must be willing to stand alone. Most of us prefer to insulate ourselves deep within the pack. Someone said, "I used to be lost in the shuffle, now I just shuffle along with the lost!"

Small minds talk about people; average minds talk about events; big minds talk about ideas. It is said of Abraham Lincoln that he paid his critics no mind. You can tell how well you're doing by the number of detractors you have. Many people seek to excuse their own lethargy by hurling lances at those who dare to dream big. Somewhere on our pilgrimage to the top we have to answer the question, "When will I stop asking myself what will others think, and start asking myself what is the right thing for me to do?"

It is lonely at the top, but for those who want to stand in the arena, as Theodore Roosevelt said, striving valiantly and, in the end, knowing the triumph of achievement, such a person must stop continually comparing themselves to others.

It's important to look ahead toward fulfilling your goals and begin today to take the path toward fulfilling them. It's far better to be a has-been than a never was! Better to go down swinging than to be called out on strikes!

10

THREE KINDS OF PEOPLE

The late columnist Earl Wilson once made the observation that we are a society made up of the haves, the have-nots, and the have-not-yet-paid-for-what-they-haves! As author Richard Foster noted, we buy things we do not need in order to impress people we do not like.

I know a woman who loves to go to garage sales. Her husband told me that she often returns carrying booty with the price tags still attached. It seems that people are consumed with consumption.

Part of the problem stems from confusion between "needs" and "wants." The more we earn, the more our wants become our supposed needs! When we're earning less than say, $30,000 a year, we don't think seriously about a trip to Europe or buying a pricey car. But let us earn what we consider to be "serious money" and suddenly we just must have that luxury pontoon boat or travel to Spain. Our wants suddenly become our needs. People go bankrupt every day trying to fill all of them.

A very successful real estate salesman I know has made a near fortune by helping people upgrade the level of their homes based on their increasing income. He works a moderate income neighborhood that abuts a middle upper-range neighborhood that is contiguous to an upper end neighborhood. He stair-steps his clients along as their financial bases grow. He told me that he came to realize that most of us think in terms of expanded purchasing power, rather than liquidation of existing debt when our income increases.

Financial expert Dave Ramsey talks about people suffering from "stuffites." More is better; newer is better; bigger is better! We buy into the subtle but destructive thinking that the one with the most toys wins. In reality, there is much profit in discipline over impulse.

> *Why do you spend money for what is not bread, And your wages for what does not satisfy? Listen carefully to Me, and eat what is good, And let your soul delight itself in abundance* (Isa. 55:2).

11

THE GENUINE ARTICLE

In Monaco, one evening, the great comedian Charlie Chaplin, whose characterization of The Little Tramp is still a classic study in humor, was gazing out over that beautiful city from his hotel balcony when his eyes caught sight of a nearby theater marquee. Emblazoned in big bold letters was an announcement that the theater would hold a Charlie Chaplin look-alike-contest the next evening.

Chaplin, who was on vacation at the time, thought it might be amusing to enter the contest. The next day he put on his make-up, grabbed his funny little hat and cane, and was off to the theater. He entered the contest but only came in third!

It is critical that we learn how to identify the genuine articles in life because there are wolves in sheep's clothing ready to exploit our ignorance. It's a blind sheep that comes to the wolf's sermon. The wrong leader can cost us money, time, or even our very lives!

Those who are skilled in spotting counterfeit money do not make an exhaustive study of the many forms of bogus bills in circulation to prepare themselves for their jobs. Rather, they become so thoroughly familiar with the genuine article that a bogus bill is immediately evident to them.

To search out truth takes effort but its reward is wisdom. When we know that we know that we know, like the experts who can spot counterfeit money, we cannot be misled.

Wisdom is known by her children, but we cannot pass on something we ourselves do not possess. The best thing a parent can do for their children is first become wise themselves. When we can divide truth from half-truths, fiction, and fantasy, we can then bestow upon our children the power of discernment

12

WHAT'S ON YOUR MIND?

Has your mind ever been tattooed with a label put there by a well-meaning parent, grandparent, friend, or teacher that hobbles you today?

I remember a story my friend, the late Dr. Norman Vincent Peale once told me. While in Singapore on a speaking assignment, he decided one evening to take a walk and enjoy the local culture. As he ambled along, he happened by a tattoo parlor. Displayed in the window were illustrations of the tattoos one could order. There was one particularly offensive image that evoked an irrepressible curiosity in Dr. Peale. He wondered who would ever have such a thing emblazoned on their body. After engaging the shop owner in some friendly conversation, he asked him this very question. Without hesitation, the shop owner replied, "Oh, they have that tattooed on their mind long before they ever come in to have it put on their body!"

Our minds are sometimes tattooed by what others say or think. It is the wise man indeed who overcomes them. No less a personage than Thomas Edison was referred to as "stupid" by one of his teachers. The great Walt Disney was once dismissed as a "dreamer." The decision to jettison such epithets is ours alone. People will accept us at our own subliminal evaluation of ourselves. Self-confidence cannot be faked for long. Low self-evaluation will manifest itself through sweaty palms, lack of eye contact, or in some cases, an over-reaching in an attempt to project self-confidence.

Self-acceptance is internal; self-confidence is external. Self-acceptance precedes self-confidence. These two qualities, in combination, give a person the grace to stand among paupers or alongside kings. If people don't like us for who we are, they surely won't like us for who we're pretending to be.

If we were misinformed as to our worth, the good news is there is hope; we can break out of the cage that the harmful words of others have put in us and be free to soar!

13

Little Dog/Big Dog

Within each of us, there lives a little dog and a big dog. The little dog is exemplified by generosity, compassion, and what Lincoln referred to as the higher angels of our nature. We are quite capable of doing selfless things, even noble things, when our world-view is turned outward toward others. But that attitude must be helped from above, because it doesn't happen naturally.

American psychologist Abraham Maslow spent his life unsuccessfully attempting to prove that man is inherently good. But one has only to observe two preschoolers vying for the same toy. Before long a big dog will assert itself and "might will try and make right."

The big dog's world-view is inwardly focused. It attempts to exercise its will over others, and its creed is: "Me first; my way!" Given the right set of circumstances, we unleash our big dog and then stand dismayed at our own harshness and lack of civility. How else could we possibly explain the actions of an otherwise reasonable, law-abiding, moderate individual who gets caught up in road rage that claims another person's life? What causes the big dog in us to snarl and bite? Is it the result of an indwelling depravity in our nature? Those who study such things claim that it is, and that the battle for dominance between the little dog and the big dog is a lifelong contest.

The little dog represents our higher nature; a nature designed to be a little lower than the angels. Saint Paul, who has had more books written about him than any other figure in history, with the exception of Jesus Christ, said, "The things I should do I do not do, and the things I do not want to do, I do! O wretched man that I am, who will save me from this body of death?" But mercifully he doesn't leave us wondering what to do. He answers his own question in the next verse: "Thanks be to God—through Jesus Christ our Lord! There is now no condemnation for those who are in Christ Jesus" (Rom. 7:19,24-25; 8-1).

We can be victorious with help from above!

14

A MOST DESTRUCTIVE STING

Every man, woman, and child is born with a weapon that can cause pain and death as surely as any cobra or black widow spider bite. Although this poison works slowly, its effect is almost always irreversible. In some cases, the one injecting the venom is totally unaware of the destruction and loss they are causing. This weapon destroys people's reputations and character rather than their lives. The weapon is the tongue, and the toxic venom that it delivers is gossip.

Gossip has no regard for correctness. It breaks hearts and ruins lives. It is devious and shrewd, yet so appealing to our human nature. Most of all, it is intrinsically malicious and grows in strength with age. The more its stories are quoted, the more acceptable as truth they become. This viper flourishes everywhere. Those who feel its sting are helpless to protect themselves. It is impossible to apprehend this virulent enemy; the harder one tries, the more elusive it becomes. Gossip has no friends. Once it stains a reputation, restoration is almost impossible because one of gossip's lingering aftereffects is doubt. Gossip sabotages governments, splinters churches, and shatters marriages. It devastates careers and causes sleepless nights, grief, and dismay. It spawns distrust and divides the closest of friends. It makes the innocent weep with despair. Gossip hisses like the viper it is.

Gossip has many faces. There is office gossip, shop gossip, church gossip, and club gossip. Gossip makes newspaper headlines and feeds the hungry social grapevine. It consumes those who have little else to occupy their minds. Before we repeat a tale let us ask ourselves: "Is it true?" "Is it fair?" "Is it important that others know?" If not, then let us stand silent.

Bless the person who, having nothing to say, remains silent rather than speaking and giving irrefutable evidence of the fact.

15

CLUB CHURCH

People attend church for many different reasons. For some, it seems like the proper thing to do, and others may see it as good for their business. It can become a kind of holy country club where we fulfill a presupposed sense of obligation while mingling with decent people. The atmosphere there can be terribly inoffensive as long as demands are not imposed. Some people pursue the God they want, instead of the God who is. They sense a need for God, but on their own terms. It's this kind of counterfeit spirituality that provoked Emerson to say that "God builds his temple in the heart of man upon the ruins of churches and religions." Church can be a dangerous place because there are few wounds that go deeper than that of being "iced" by our brothers and/or sisters in the Lord.

But church can also be a wonderful place. Serious seekers primarily attend church for two reasons: to worship God and to have their needs met. The earnest caretaker of his soul is far more zealous about the *heart* of veneration than the *art* of veneration.

The quest for a church that instructs and teaches uncompromising truth is worth the search because only in truth is there light, and only in light is there life. Great church life brings freedom and freedom brings joy. Joy is quite different than happiness. Joy is internal, based on a deep sense of eternal security and doesn't evaporate like a puff of smoke.

Many kinds of churches are available today. This permits some to mollify their troubled conscience, but the church that is composed of members who seek to better know God is one that will bring its members great joy.

16

DEALING WITH ANGER

"Yeah, I lose my temper, but it's all over in a minute," the man confessed. His friend replied, "So is the hydrogen bomb, but think of the damage it produces!"

In his book, *The Man in the Mirror,* Patrick Morley writes, "Anger destroys the quality of our personal lives, our health, and our marriages."

Anger is predominantly caused by self-centeredness and impatience. When people are so focused on themselves, they are apt to erupt into anger anytime someone disagrees with them or cannot move as fast as them.

Some people are perfectionists and cannot accept the fact that others will make mistakes. Sometimes they feel guilty when they have erred themselves and tend to quickly take it out on others.

Still others have experienced deep seated traumas and react to the slightest provocation with anger because they have never completely dealt with their original trauma.

Anger can take on different forms with different people. With some it is a quiet cold rejection of the other person and with others it is a flaming outburst that destroys everything and everyone in its path.

The results of anger are never good. People have developed ulcers from it—either as perpetrators or as victims. Heart attacks and strokes have been documented to follow an intense outburst of anger and, on the other hand, from anger smoldering within for years.

The one who can control his anger is the one who displays uncommon strength.

17

CROSSES WE BEAR

Two thousand years ago, criminals in Rome were forced to carry their own crosses to the execution site in order to signify their submission to Rome's power. Today, many of us are forced to carry crosses we did not seek either. Sometimes our trials are so burdensome that no one this side of heaven can help us. During these times, heroic effort is needed, moment by moment, just to carry on.

We should presume that our live will be filled with nothing but contentment because most of life's major course changes are unplanned. All kinds of disasters can happen and we should not be caught flat-footed by it or, on the other hand, live in a state of perpetual fear.

We need divine intervention to extricate us from our despair. The first century Roman philosopher

Seneca said, "All my life I have been seeking to climb out of the pit, and I cannot do it unless a hand is let down to draw me up."

Roy Campanella, the star catcher for the old Brooklyn Dodgers, learned how to do this while laying in a hospital room recovering from an automobile accident. One day a mother brought her young son to see the great catcher and ask if he would autograph a baseball for him. Campanella, in the depths of discouragement over the end of his stellar career, declined and said that his hand shook so badly the boy wouldn't be able to read it. "That's okay, Mr. Campanella," the young boy replied, "I'm blind anyway." Roy said that was the day he stopped feeling sorry for himself.

18

DEGENERATION

Everything eventually wears out because it's the natural progression of things. If you park a new automobile in the middle of a field and leave it there, it will eventually disintegrate. A home or farm left unattended will crumble over time. In much the same way, people wear out.

In my twenties I had no understanding of this and thought my legs would always be strong and my lungs would allow me to run forever. As the clock ticks down, we become more physically limited. Now, when I get up in the morning and find that my knees are working well, I think it's going to be a pretty good day.

There is another form of degeneration that can happen at any age, but it does not stem from physical or mental decline, it has to do with the inner man—the spirit of a person. This degeneration happens when self becomes king and pride becomes our master. We throw off all restraint and accountability, substituting our search for pleasure. We do what feels good or seems right. Feelings make for accommodating servants but deceitful masters.

We all need some kind of moral standard by which to measure ourselves. The Bible is the one enduring book that contains all the truth we will ever need for life, health, wealth, and true happiness.

It also helps to have someone who's older and wiser to mentor us. The experiences they share may help us avoid making some of the same mistakes that they did. But if we seek advice or a sense of direction from someone who lacks wisdom, we'll be like a blind man following another—we'll both will fall into the ditch. We must be careful to surround ourselves with people of integrity if we wish to mature in our daily life.

19

FOUR RULES TO LIVE BY

Most people today probably don't remember Elsa Maxwell, but in the 1950s she was very much a part of the social merry-go-round in our nation's capital. Her parties were legendary.

She once told her friend, former late-night talk show host Jack Paar, that her dying father gave her four rules to live by. After studying them, I have found them to be of immense value in my own life.

Here are the rules a young woman learned from a wise father:

1) Don't compare yourself to others.

2) Don't be afraid of "They," for "They" are a collection of "You's and Me's."

3) Be in work you like and be with people you like; work hard and play hard.

4) The more you own, the more you are possessed by it, because the more you have to maintain.

We can most assuredly learn from others; it's a way to reduce the "timeline" to worthwhile productivity. On the other hand, to constantly compare ourselves to others leads only to despair or arrogance. Magnifying the abilities of others while minimizing our own, or looking with disdain and counterfeit compassion upon others around us is the way of the insecure.

Being continually concerned about what others think serves only to hamstring us. In trying to please everyone, we please no one. High achievers understand the profundity of the Latin exhortation, *Ille iter accelerat qui itus solus*: He runs fastest who runs alone. Achieving anything monumental by a committee is a little like herding cats.

Finally, the more we free ourselves from "things," the freer we will be indeed! We need to recall the old maxim that reminds us that we come into life with clenched fists and go out with open hands.

20

HOW TO BE A THOUGHTFUL HUSBAND

I don't think I have ever met a woman who does not like either chocolate or flowers. And for wives, there is a third thing that ranks equally high—the anticipation of their needs and desires by their husbands.

An insightful anecdote appeared in the *Wall Street Journal* recently about Cokey Roberts, co-anchor of the ABC program *This Week With Sam Donaldson and Cokey Roberts.* She said her husband of 35 years, Steve Roberts, a commentator on public television's *Washington Week In Review* and CNN's *Late Edition*, was getting better at doing the things she asks him to do, but that he still has not learned to anticipate the things she needs done. This is one of the major lessons we have to learn as husbands. It is only with the heart that one sees clearly things unperceived by a preoccupied mind.

Anticipation is the highest kind of service. There are three other levels of service: Hide-and-seekers, surrenderers, and volunteers. The classical example of hide-and-seekers are the department store clerks who ignore us. If we become persistent in our attempts to capture their attention and finally corner them, they have zero options left and must move to the second level of service—surrender. Begrudgingly, they must concede that we represent the profit in this encounter and set about to help us. The third level of service is volunteers. These type of people have a healthy and cheerful approach and really make the effort to serve us. These are the people whom you like to tip well.

Clearly though, the level of service for someone like an administrative assistant who works with an executive day after day, or a husband with a modicum of sensitivity, is that of anticipation. They should strive to always meet, as best they can, the unspoken needs of the other person in the relationship.

21

I WONDER...

The unimaginable happenings of September 11, 2001 have shaken to the core every American. As a result Bible sales are up, and more people are attending church. This got me to thinking about the spiritual relevance of these events.

Like Israel 3500 years ago, we seem to cycle repetitiously through the same phases: rejection of things spiritual, bitter sorrows or fear, contrite reflection and rededication, and then reinstatement and favor.

It's like the person who fails to take care of their health until it breaks. They readjust their priorities, make a decision to live healthier, and then once recovered, drift back into destructive behavior.

As children, most of us experienced correction by our fathers. We are also corrected, I believe, by an eternal Father who has our best interests at heart. Without claiming to be a prophet, I wonder if God isn't using the terrorists to shake up our thinkers, much as He used Nebuchadnezzar to chasten the Israelites of old. God declares that He is a jealous God. But His jealously is not a result of insecurity as much as out of protective concern for us.

Here again, I wonder if we have grown so self-sufficient that we have built monuments to our wealth and power, much as in antiquity when the people decided to build a tower that would reach the heavens. The tower of Babel was to be a monument to themselves.

We all witnessed, on September 11, the vulnerability of our modern-day edifices. We cannot put our faith exclusively in finite things. Three days after the tragedy, the Presidential prayer service was broadcast from Washington's National Cathedral. As the many high-ranking dignitaries arrived it was gloomy, dark and rainy; but as they emerged from the building, the sun was brightly shining. I wonder if it was a sign.

22

INTERPRET, DON'T REACT

There's a wonderful story told about the late Bishop Fulton J. Sheen. While traveling, he once found himself confronted by a waitress in a hotel coffee shop who liked everything about her job except the people she had to serve. With less than feigned interest, she asked him what he wanted to order for breakfast. "Two eggs over easy, a glass of juice, an order of toast...and a kind word," he replied good-naturedly.

A short time later she returned, perfunctorily placed the food before him, turned on her heels and walked off. The good bishop called after her inquiring about his kind word. Without missing a step she growled over her shoulder, "Don't eat them eggs!"

We can learn valuable information from people that are rude or even dislike us. These people will tell us things even our best friends won't share for fear of hurting our feelings. The key is to intellectually and unemotionally interpret what they say rather than react to it, although our natural tendency is to strike back.

Today, with characters in popular sit-coms indulging in cute but sarcastic put-downs, we have raised "striking-back" in our society to an art form. However, a closed mouth gathers no foot. Or, as my dear old father used to say, "Kill 'em with kindness." You cannot lose if you follow that advice. If a nasty remark comes from an adversary, never give them the satisfaction of knowing that what they said pierced you. If it comes from a friend or business acquaintance, you can simply ignore the remark and avoid jeopardizing a valued relationship.

Interpreting rather than reacting is the exemplification of self-control and is achieved through confidence in who we are and the assurance of our relationship. In a rambunctious and uptight society, it is a rare commodity.

23

KNOW YOUR FLAG

Most people, I would think, know that the 13 stripes in our nation's flag represent the original states. Also, most people can tell you that the stars represent the states of the Union. But what do the colors mean?

At this time when our country finds itself engaged in bringing liberty on the other side of the world, the colors of our flag not only remind us of our precious freedom won by blood, sweat, and tears, but also entreat us to make whatever sacrifices are necessary in order to ensure that liberty prevails elsewhere.

The *red* in the flag represents courage. Proverbs 24:10 says that "if you falter in times of trouble, how small is your strength!" In Jeremiah 12:5 it asks, "If you have raced with men on foot and they have worn you out, how can you compete with horses? If you stumble in safe country, how will you manage in the thickets by the Jordan?" In other words, if you can't handle difficulties in the easy times, what will you do in the days of calamity?

White represents purity and innocence. Innocence does not mean naiveté, but rather purity of motives. For example, we have never striven to colonize other peoples in other lands, but only to aid them in their time of need.

Blue represents justice, perseverance, and vigilance. Perhaps now, more than at any time in our history, we must persevere and be more vigilant, not only as a nation, but also as individuals.

Centuries ago, many sophisticated leaders in Rome underestimated the rugged Asian hordes wanting to pull down her gates. We should not tremble or cower at the thought of terrorism in our house, but at the same time it would be madness to dismiss the efforts of the terrorists as futile because, in fact, they are capable adversaries.

In striving to fulfill the wonderful qualities the colors of our flag represent, it would be immature to live only with the ideal and ignore reality. But to live only in reality and fail to reach for the ideal would be to exist under a banner of hollow symbols.

24

MAINTAINING A LIGHTER SIDE

Although the world is made up of many nationalities, religions, and political persuasions, all humans on the face of the earth do two things exactly alike: cry and laugh. There are different cultural factors that trigger these emotions, but a person doesn't cry in Chinese or Swahili. A hearty Germanic laughter is indistinguishable from a boisterous North American laughter.

Laughter can cleanse and purify the soul, both for the individual and the nation. To have the emotional strength to laugh at oneself can be a contributing factor to good health. Just as worry causes rotting in the bones, laughter brings restoration. Sometimes we have no choice but to laugh at the contradictions of life.

Only in America...

- Can a pizza get to your house faster than the police.

• Are there handicap-parking places in front of a skating rink.

• Do people order double cheeseburgers and large fries along with a diet drink.

• Do banks leave their front doors wide open and chain their pens to the countertops.

• Do we leave cars, costing thousands of dollars, parked in the driveway, and keep useless, worn-out things protected in the garage.

• Do we rigorously exercise and afterwards reward ourselves with high calorie food and/or drink.

• Do we spend money for an expensive scale to monitor our weight and then avoid looking at it.

25

A Small Key To Big Time Savings

Someone once said that the best way to determine whom you should spend the majority of your time with is to think of the people who will attend your funeral.

There are "fair weather friends," and there are "true friends." As we sojourn through life, many people will want to come alongside. Unfortunately many of them will be interested only in what they can gain from having a relationship with us.

Keeping in mind that we can control how we relate to the people in our lives, here is a simple three-step process for handling one of life's peskiest chores—answering our phone messages!

The first group consists of people who are entitled to a *good shot.* They will receive a return phone call or e-mail at our convenience. We might respond today, tomorrow, or several days from now. High productivity people don't let other people's emergencies become their urgencies.

The second classification is made up of people deserving of a *better shot.* Maximizing the efficacy of this step, we can batch our calls together and return inquiries or e-mails at a predecided time. A sincere effort would be made to contact all of them by day's end. This second step precludes a never-ending string of interruptions that stalls our momentum and keeps us from accomplishing our appointed tasks.

The third classification of people gets our *best shot.* These people receive a return contact from us immediately, or as soon as we can break free from what preoccupies us. Hopefully this would always include our mates and our children! I know people who would put the President of the United States on hold if one of their kids called, for they know that, in all probability, the President will not be attending their funeral.

26

THE RESTLESS HEART

Throughout the ages, men have always looked for happiness or satisfaction through sensual gratification, the acquisition of material things, or ascendancy to power. Living life on these levels ends in vanity, futility, and exhaustion.

In the book of Ecclesiastes, King Solomon gives testimony from his own life that all pursuits as an end in themselves end in dissatisfaction. After drinking from this cup, Solomon viewed human wisdom and effort with skepticism.

Many look upon this book in the Bible as portraying how bleak and pessimistic life is, but such a view is like the man describing a half glass of liquid as being half empty. While the book surely does condemn a materialistic interpretation of life, the writer is showing us a glass half full. He is in essence saying, one way is easy as we glide along, but we eventually will wind up in a heap. The alternative path is narrow and uphill that at first seems extremely difficult but becomes increasingly easier as we settle into the yoke of the great Shepherd (Matt. 11:28-30).

Many of us are careless about the stewardship of the precious gift of life given to us by our Creator. Some plaintively live out their days not unlike French playwright Jean Paul Sartre who said, "There is no exit from this meaningless existence." In truth, God is in charge of the exits.

The problem is that today we don't accept absolutes. Modern man is of the mind that everything is relative. In our richness as a society we tend to survey all that our small strength has acquired, and say, as Nebuchadnezzar, Monarch of Babylon, said while standing on his balcony overlooking Babylon, "Look what my hands have wrought." God made his nails to grow and he spend a season of time lowing like a cow and eating grass, until he acknowledged the God of the universe who had blessed him abundantly.

27

DO-IT-YOURSELF PROJECT

There is an arrogant assertion of human independence today. We think very highly of independence in this country,. It's a distinct privilege to live and work in a land of the free and the brave. But in things eternal it's a life of dependence that insures security.

When an automaker wants to study a certain make or model of a competitor they purchase one and take it apart piece by piece and catalog every nut and bolt. This practice is known as benchmarking.

Life is a much more complex creation than an automobile. Only a nitwit would attempt to complete a long trip without first being familiar with his vehicle: gas mileage, tyre pressure, how the global positioning system operates, etc.

If automakers are so interested in knowing how to build a better car, and buyers will spend considerable time familiarizing themselves with the owners manual of their new automobile, something that will last a relatively short time, does it not make sense to consult the owners manual written by the Master builder himself? The Bible is not a history book, although it describes a lot of interesting history, it is most of all a book on how to live.

Life is a do-it-yourself project. Our lives today are the result of our attitudes and choices of the past. Our lives tomorrow will be the result of the attitudes and choices we make today.

Unless the Lord builds a house, they labor in vain who build it (Psalm 127:1).

28

TODAY'S HEROES

There are three things that can be said for so many of today's heroes: 1) They are media made, 2) They are money driven, and 3) Their fame is momentary. Their high status in society is based on their current popularity and not on the depth of their philosophy. For some unfathomable reason, we seem to grant them extra influence and authority. Someone who is a star tennis player is asked about his or her views concerning Bangladesh. Or some actor thinks their expertise exceeds that of the current administration regarding a Middle Eastern conflict.

Real heroes are not made or created by a system. A system will use you, abuse you, and confuse you. They will use you as a tool to get what they want, usually money, but in some cases, power or personal favors. They will abuse you by depleting your energies until you can no longer serve them in gaining their ends. They will confuse you, sometimes not intentionally, by fashioning a myth, which we then begin to believe.

If we are a created hero, the system will discard us when we lose our value to it because our beauty fades, our skill diminishes, or our age takes its toll on our mental capabilities. If our security lies in how famous we are or what we know rather than resting secure in the One who created us, we will have nothing to live for when our strengths leave us, when we can no longer carry the ball, run down the court, or draw the crowds.

Fame is fleeting but the drive for it can be so subtle as to be imperceptible. Real heroes don't measure their standing by the appraisal of others. They trust God and not their emotions or feelings. Although some, like great military leaders, can have towering egos, most are quiet and unassuming. For example, how many names of Medal of Honor recipients do you know? By the depth of their character, which includes an uncommon but ingrained sense of selflessness, they responded in times of crisis and made a difference.

29

ALL SIZES AND SHAPES

Heroes come in all shapes, sizes, genders, colors, races, and ages. I remember Mohammed Ali, the great prizefighter, climbing up to a ledge and talking a young man from jumping to his death. I think of Audie Murphy, the most decorated soldier of World War II, climbing atop a burning tank and manning a machine gun to drive off an advancing enemy.

Then there was General William Dean, highest-ranking American prisoner to be captured in Korea, swatting 40,671 flies, and counting every one them, in order to stave off boredom and loneliness, writing what his captors said would be his last letter home to tell his young son, Bill Jr. about integrity. And I think of General Douglas MacArthur, the American Caesar, whose name is still to this day called out in the ranks of the Philippine army during roll call.

But I also think of the quiet heroes who fight against hatred and discrimination. And I think of a ball player for the New York Yankees by the name of Lou Gehrig who showed his greatest courage off the field, fighting a losing battle with multiple sclerosis. There's also former President Ronald Reagan heading into the oblivion of Alzheimer's, having filled his place in history by helping to end the cold war. I think of the fire fighters and police who gave the greatest sacrifice on a fall day in 2001—a sunny day that turned into ashen darkness.

I think of the military that stands guard, ready to defend us. I think of all the underpaid—at any salary—school teachers who will probably never know the difference they have made in the lives of so many children. And the millions of people who quietly carry out their appointed duties, trying everyday to do the very best they can.

These are the real heroes.

30

In Pursuit of Wholeness

SNARES THAT TEAR

A big part of the major problem we face today is the same as in the time of Judges in the Old Testament: "In those days there was no king in Israel, so every man did what was right in his own eyes" (Judges 17:6). In the 21st century, truth is relevant, and tolerance is looked upon as having greater value than absolutes. It is like a ship trying to get out of the harbor with no captain, navigator, or helmsman aboard.

WOUNDS AND MEDICATION

We have all been subjected to the slings and arrows of life, but wounds from friends go deeper than social slights and can be much more difficult to heal. These wounds can cripple us emotionally, causing us to medicate ourselves in ways that become self-destructive. But there is hope; there is One who can reverse what the canker worm has eaten. He can help us extend forgiveness to others and in return receive healing for our souls.

FANTASY

Fantasy keeps reality at a distance. Fantasy is an escape, and escapes can be either harmless or dangerous. There is no harm in escaping for a while through a hobby or other harmless pastime in order to ease the tensions of a pressure-cooker life. But anything taken to an extreme becomes a liability. Fantasy is illusion that can sweep us along like partygoers rafting down a swift river, unaware of its power and the falls that lie ahead.

CONFUSION AND DISCOURAGEMENT

When we are confused or discouraged we become extremely vulnerable. Confusion can result from not knowing what to believe or whom to believe. These two demons can cause great discomfort and stress. Coupled with our penchant for quick fixes, they can make us susceptible to having our ears tickled to hear what we want to hear and ignore the truth.

DENIAL

Denial of our weaknesses is caused by our fear of being rejected, abandoned, or blacklisted. Admission of weakness is contemptible in a society that prides itself on its strengths. The most destructive form of denial is self-denial. With eyes wide shut, we commit suicide in slow doses.

SHAME AND GUILT

Shame and guilt can be healthy or unhealthy. One can bring renewed life, the other prolonged death. False shame can cause us to assume phony identities in order to avoid more hurt and render us unable to accept forgiveness from others or even God. The ultimate tragedy of shame is that it grows like a cancer, even until death. Guilt, on the other hand, if dealt with properly by seeking God's and man's forgiveness, can bring us the peace and joy we so desperately need.

SURRENDER

Unlike military surrender, spiritual surrender is voluntary. Surrender is one of the most difficult things for us to do. Man wants to be self-reliant, so we have an inherent tendency to reject any authority that would rule over us. Yet, surrender to God must come before we can ever experience true freedom.

THE WILDERNESS

The wilderness is a terribly lonely place to be, but anyone who experienced it comes away realizing that it can provide them with new strength. To lie quietly and patiently upon the altar of self-sacrifice, one must prevent the will from running riot.

GETTING REAL – THE 30-DAY MAKEOVER

Cosmetic Christianity—trying to be good on the outside—will wear you out. Real change isn't easy, but then, nothing of eternal value is.

TRANSPARENCY

Spiritual transparency is central to our relationship with God. Transparency is based on mutual trust. If we trust the wrong people and reveal ourselves to them, it is like handing an enemy a loaded gun with which to hold us captive. But true liberation from a distorted "system" of life is worth the search for those we can truly trust.

31

MORE GOLD NUGGETS LEARNED ALONG THE WAY

Opportunity is sometimes spelled RISK, and risk is sometimes spelled FOOLISH! At times we must be willing to fall down and appear foolish in the eyes of others.

Life is too short to give ourselves to an inferior purpose.

Our country's answer lies not in guided missiles, but in guided men.

Goethe was correct when he said, "They who do nothing for others do nothing for themselves."

There is no smaller package on earth than someone who is all wrapped up in themselves.

You have no friend or ally in someone who will not share a truth.

The major course changes in life are unplanned. The

great lessons of life are learned in adversity.

We either love things and use people, or we love people and use things.

Being poor is nothing if we have everything, and great wealth is nothing if that's all we have.

The person having fun will always outperform or outsell the person who works merely out of a sense of duty.

We should strive not so much to be good, but to be effective.

It is better to receive wounds from a friend than kisses from an enemy.

There is eternal wisdom in what Grove Patterson, the great Editor of the *Toledo Blade* newspaper once said—the Architect of the universe didn't build a stairway leading nowhere.

SILVER BULLETS

...for Your Career

32

A UNIQUE BREED

Not too long ago in Carlisle, England, I was scheduled to hold a seminar for a group of sales people. Before walking into the meeting room, I noticed an interesting note posted on their message board that read:

> The company regrets that it has come to our attention that salespeople are dying on the job and failing to fall down. This practice must stop as it becomes impossible to distinguish between death and normal movement of the staff. In the future any salesperson found dead in an upright position will be dropped from the company registry!

Salespeople, especially those on full commission, are a unique breed. They're like a finely tuned racing engine. They experience higher highs and lower lows than most of us. They live in hotels and motels, on airplanes, in buses, cars, and cabs. They correct more errors, explain more discrepancies, bear more disappointments, and pacify more belligerent customers than any group of people including ministers. They introduce more new goods, dispose of more old goods, load more trucks and rail cars, unload more ships, start more new businesses, and write more debits and credits in our ledgers than any other group in America.

They are the most well-rounded individuals because they must be able to converse with such a wide variety of people. The majority of salespeople are dedicated, disciplined, and well-trained. They are the oil of the free enterprise engine. No truck will pull out of the depot, no ship leave port, no passenger or cargo plane taxi to the runway for take-off, but first a sale has been made! As the late editor of *Parade* magazine, Red Motley, once said, "Nothing happens in this country until somebody sells something!"

Here's to these warm, wonderful people—you're doing a great job!

33

ADDED VALUE

It never ceases to amaze me how many companies fail to realize that the person answering the phone represents the entire company. Too many companies put a novice in this important position. I once overheard a bank receptionist tell a customer on the phone that the person they were trying to reach was "out of their cage." How odd this must have sounded to the caller if they were not familiar with bank jargon.

It is five times easier to keep a current customer than to win a new one. I purchased a suit once that I had to take back five times before they got the alterations right. I never went back to that store again. If they had given me a tie or gift certificate to assuage my exasperation, I would probably still be a client today. The difference between a client and a customer is that a client spends more money because they keep returning on a regular basis.

It brings to rememberance the story about two candy stores located the very same distance from an elementary school. One store was failing; the other store was doing a thriving business. When the kids came into the failing store and asked for a pound of candy, the owner would put a scoop of candy on the scales, then keep taking some off until the right amount was indicated. The owner of the second store, on the other hand, would purposefully keep from putting enough candy on the scales, then, with great showmanship, keep adding more and more until the right amount was reached. To the kids it looked like they were getting more candy at the second store. Added value can be "perceived" value! The first store failed; the second store is still going strong.

34

"CARGO CULT" MENTALITY

During World War II, the pilot of a military transport became disoriented and dropped the plane's cargo on an island outside the war zone. The natives who inhabited the island, not being accustomed to hearing the roar of aircraft engines overhead, came running out of their huts. Looking up, they were startled to see the sky full of parachutes. Converging on the cache as it hit the ground, they discovered many things they could put to good use. It is said that every day thereafter, at exactly the same time, they would come streaming out of their little huts and look up, waiting expectantly for more manna from heaven.

"Cargo Cult" mentality says, I'm going to invest very little, if anything, and look for a big pay-off to fall out of the sky. Three examples of people with a cargo-cult mentality in our society today are those who play the lottery, those who are waiting to receive their inheritance, and those who play the slot machines. Nothing may ever float down from the sky to them.

Not too long ago, a banker told me that he had turned down a loan request from a good customer who had a great idea for a copycat fast food restaurant. The banker said that people today are so conditioned to instant everything, that they expect success to come in the same way. The man might have had a good idea, but he hadn't spent time planning it out and doing the necessary research to see if it was a viable idea before he approached the banker.

There's an old proverb that says: "Those who cut wood are thrice warmed. They are warmed when they cut it, warmed when they carry it, and warmed when they burn it."

Today, many people don't want to cut or carry any wood. As my old friend Earl Nightingale would say, that's like the man who sat in front of the stove and said, "Give me heat, then I'll add the wood!"

Getting wisdom is the most important thing you can do! (Prov.. 4:7).

35

CONFRONTATION: GOOD OR BAD?

During leadership conferences at which I am a speaker, I sometimes ask people what thoughts come to their mind when I say the word "confrontation." They usually respond with words like stress, opposition, tension, conflict, and fight. Most everyone, at least in these seminars, seems to have a misconception about confrontation. Confrontation is neutral; it's how it's handled that makes it good or bad. The whole point in confronting someone is to settle an issue and get back to productivity. When strife is present, unity loses its power.

We see a greater number of confrontations today because we are a more litigious society. This all began in the 1960s. Prior to this time, society ranked higher than the individual. Today, the individual ranks higher than society and uses it to his/her advantage. Great minds that study these things say that in the 60s we were into self-gratification. In the 70s we were into self-indulgence. In the 80s it was self-centeredness. In the 90s we looked for self-fulfillment. With the focus on self for four decades, there is little wonder we are quick to take exception when somebody crosses us or rubs us the wrong way.

We are super-sensitive today about being wronged. Arbitrations, litigations, and judicial appeals clog our legal system. We want justice as we perceive it to be.

We need to keep in mind that no one is made of glass and that no one has X-ray vision. Communication will go a long way in helping us prevent breakdowns in our relationships. A wise saying counsels, "All seems so right until the other side is heard. Do not be hasty to argue your case lest your foe put you to shame."

Try to settle your differences peaceably, for winners never really win because losers never forget. It is to a person's credit to avoid strife and turmoil; only fools want to rage and scoff.

I am leaving you with a gift—peace of mind and heart! And the peace I give isn't fragile like the peace the world gives (John 14:27).

36

FOCUSING FOR RESULTS

One of the things that always fascinated me as a kid was the lion tamer at the circus. I couldn't figure out how he could control the big cat and keep from being mauled. I discovered later that outside of making sure the lion was well fed, the secret to his safety lay not in the whip, but the chair. By keeping the legs of the chair pointed at the big cat he confused it by presenting it with too many targets. Not knowing which leg to attack first, the animal remained threatening but hesitant.

With an endless array of choices, we can sometimes react like that lion. When we fail to focus on a specific target, we never generate enough momentum to accomplish much. Confused or distracted, we select the easy option and elect to sit in a comfortable in front of the television set, watching other people make an excellent living while we scrimp to get by.

Movies can be another way to wile away the future. I know of a person who saw "Titanic" eight times! I can't help but wonder what he missed the first seven times. Of course, enjoying relaxation time in a tense world is healthy. We all need good mini breaks, but anything good taken to an extreme becomes a weakness. The question is: "Are we fishing in life or merely maintaining an aquarium?"

We could take any subject—flowers, plants, planets, the American revolution, investing in mutual funds, the Bible—and study everything we could find on the topic, and at the end of 90 days, know more about that subject than 98% of the people alive in the world today!

Last year, we spent over ten billion dollars on antiperspirants. Many people look good and smell good, but don't work hard enough to need one.

Here is my final conclusion: fear God and obey his commandments, for this is the entire duty of man (Ecclesiastes 12:13).

37

CORRECTION THAT DOESN'T KILL

While it is true that all of us, from time to time, need a good swift kick in the direction of our potential, it's how it's administered that determines whether it leads to our cooperation or resentment. As we're all aware, resentment can lead to tragic consequences.

A wise parent never disciplines a child in order to vent their own anger; a wise leader, manager, or supervisor never does either! This is significant because we get back what we sow. If we reduce people to pulp, we get back more bad behavior, spurred on by resentment.

Here is a simple seven-step formula to insure future cooperation with the correction we administer:

1. Do it with the other person's best interests at heart.

2. Do it in private. No one likes to be dressed down and embarrassed in front of others.

3. Preface your correction with a kind word—something that lets them know they are of value.

4) Criticize the act and not the person. This is pivotal, because it's at this point that we either win future cooperation or birth an adversary.

5) Tell the person how it should have been done. It is patently wrong to call someone into accountability if they don't know what is expected of them or what the correct procedure is.

6) Ask for their cooperation. Make sure you have eye contact when you ask. Unless a person is an inveterate liar, it is very difficult to disregard an agreement.

7) Part on a friendly note. This can be done verbally or with a touch. Whether a pat on the back, shoulder, arm, or just a simple handshake, it says, "I still accept you unconditionally."

> *I didn't want to hurt you, but I had to show you how very much I loved you and cared about what was happening to you.* (2 Corinthians 2:4).

38

DxVxTFS=C

There's a startling statement in the Bible that says, "Without a vision the people perish." This is true not only regarding the spiritual, but our material fortunes as well.

Before people will take action to change, two conditions have to exist: they must be dissatisfied and, they must have vision or perception. DxVxTFS=C means Dissatisfaction times Vision times Taking the First Step equals Change.

There are people who are dissatisfied, but they have no vision or insight, and therefore, no change will take place in their lives. Some people reject vision because they are afraid that they will be held accountable for it. Others simply lack the ability to envision change.

Such was the case with a man many years ago. In a Sunday morning service, his preacher said that one day people would fly like birds from place to place. This man took such umbrage at what he considered to be an outrageous and seemingly heretical statement that he stood up in the middle of the assembly and exclaimed that the only ones able to fly were angels. The man continued to be so distressed that he decided to leave the church, and so he did, taking his two young sons, Orville and Wilbur with him. Thankfully, Mr. Wright's sons were not as small minded as he was.

A more recent example of lack of vision happened in 1977 when the founder and president of Digital Equipment Corporation, Ken Olson, opined that he could see no reason why anyone would want a computer in their home. Small thinking lost this man and his company a lot of time and money.

History is replete with naysayers. The mind lacking vision produces a verdict, while the creative mind produces an idea. Letting the mind soar as it was divinely designed to do opens the door to untold riches.

If you want favor with both God and man never tire of loyalty and kindness (Prov. 3:3).

39

FIGHT OR FLIGHT

Choosing your battles by weighing the costs is a sign of strength and wisdom. Knowing what's worth fighting for and when to fight is prudent. It is not cowardly to flee sometimes.—it's better to be a live dog than a dead lion, a wise proverb advocates.

In the presidential election of 1960, the Democratic Party in San Antonio, Texas decided to hold a fundraiser at the Alamo—the exemplification of everything selfless and brave.

The young senator and presidential hopeful, John Kennedy, was to be the guest speaker. On the evening of the gala affair, Kennedy leaned over halfway through the dinner to ask the mayor if there was a back way out. He explained that he had to travel to Houston for an early breakfast meeting and would like to leave a little early. The mayor looked at Kennedy and said, "Senator, if there was a back way out of here, there never would have been an Alamo!"

Sometime, somewhere, we have to burn our bridges, throw our hat over the wall, draw a line in the sand, and make a stand. Fear and doubt may be the only things that keep our achievements at a distance.

Sometimes, we need to experience the inspiration of desperation to move us off our natural inclination towards inertia. Procrastination, after all, is a decision to do nothing.

Brave hearts know that they die but once, while those who are faint-hearted die a thousand times. The brave live by faith; the faint hearted live in fear.

Speaker Sheila Bethel Murray defines true determination this way: I.W.D.I.O.I.W.D. (I Will Do It or I Will Die). When we display this kind of resolve, it conveys tremendous strength and purpose. There's something magnetic about a firm commitment in a person.

Commit your work to the Lord and your plans will be established (Prov. 16:3).

40

FOUR KINDS OF PEOPLE

We all know that V.I.P.s are Very Important People. But what are V.T.P.s? And what about V.N.P.s, or V.D.P.s?

By V.I.P.s I'm not referring to what Swiss poet, and theologian Lavater described as people who give themselves airs of importance in order to compensate for feelings of impotence. In our definition, V.I.P.s are those who encourage us, believe in us, and challenge us to be all that we can be.

V.T.P.s are very teachable or trainable people. The windows of their minds are open to new ideas and concepts. These people are a joy to be around and a delight to have on our staff. Many people like to think of themselves as V.T.P.s, but in actuality only concentrate on rearranging their prejudices.

V.N.P.s are very nice people, without a great deal going on in their lives. They spend their time talking about events or visiting memory lane. They can quote baseball statistics from thirty years ago, and quite frequently stay current with all the soap operas. They're thoroughly pleasant and folksy, but they have gotten off the train and are spending time in the station, no longer growing and going.

V.D.P.s are very draining people. These are the kind of people that stood on the bank scoffing at Fulton as he worked on his steamboat. They declared that he would never get the thing to float. When it went steaming proudly up the Hudson River in 1807, they said he would never get the boat to stop. These people are small thinkers and will drain the energy out of your emotional batteries. They brighten up a room when they walk out of it.

V.I.P.s are generous people and give of themselves. V.T.P.s are open and eager to learn and apply. V.N.P.s are nice people with whom to wile away some time. V.D.P.s will turn you into a cynic and rob you of the joy of living. Let's try and work on becoming V.I.P.s for the rest of our lives.

> *For the Holy Spirit does not want you to be afraid of people, but to be wise and strong, and to love them and enjoy being with them* (2 Timothy 1:7).

41

HABIT: SERVANT OR MASTER?

I am your constant companion. I am your greatest helper or your heaviest burden. I can push you onward and upward or drag you down to the gutter. I am at your command. Half the tasks you do might as well be turned over to me right away so I can do them quickly and correctly. I am easily managed; you must merely be firm with me. Show me exactly how you want something done, and after a few lessons I will do it automatically.

I am the servant of all successful people and, alas, of all failures as well. Those who are great, I have made great. Those who are failures, I have made failures. I am not a machine, but I work with all the precision of a machine, plus the intelligence of a person.

You may run me for profit or run me for ruin, it makes no difference to me. Take me, train me, be firm with me, and I will put the world at your feet! Be easy with me, and I will destroy you. Who am I? I am Habit.

That little story helps point out the importance of the habits we make a part of our everyday lives. We are made into slaves, someone said, not by our heredity, but by the habits bred into us in our youth. On the other hand, the achievements in our future are based on the habits we form today.

Good habits are just as difficult to break as bad ones, they're just more difficult to initially form because there's greater resistance involved. It's easier to take the line of least resistance. Once formed, however, good habits will serve us faithfully throughout our lives.

Whether it's exercise, study habits, fastening our seat belt, or setting aside a daily quiet time, good habits are like good friends—they should be persistently cultivated and never abandoned.

Don't you realize that you can choose your own master? You can choose sin (with death) or else obedience (with acquittal).

42

Honesty

The old axiom is true—honesty *is* the best policy. Truthfulness is both timeless and timely. Abraham Lincoln said if you don't lie, you won't need a good memory. Honesty is its own defense because it stands the test of time.

When ambition goes amuck, honesty can be found at odds with expediency. We have all seen people in high places brought low as a result of ignoring the need for honesty. Presidents have been impeached and their credibility has vanished because of their lies. People who consistently try to take short cuts to success short circuit their own efforts and throw away their own opportunities.

Someone said we are a nation whose second language is lying. From the seemingly innocuous, "Let's have lunch...I'll call you," with no intention of doing so, to the serious act of perjury, many conduct their affairs today with half-truths and bodacious misrepresentations. I have met only two people in my lifetime that I can say unequivocally are uncompromisingly forthright. Both of these people understand the hard truth and deep wisdom of the admonition: It is better to be poor than dishonest!

There was a young man who was being considered for a promotion to vice-presidency in a large bank. On the very day the decision was to be voted upon, the president of the bank observed the young man slip a two-cent pad of butter under the lip of his plate in the company cafeteria in order to avoid paying for it. That afternoon the president sadly confessed that he could not vote in favor of the young man. The president understood that a person who steals a piece of butter could easily steal a cow (or its equivalent in money). A person who tells a white lie is predisposed to tell a bigger one.

43

INTO REALITY

In a scene from the movie "Dirty Harry," Clint Eastwood stood at gunpoint while the malevolent police commissioner, played by Hal Holbrook, attempted to make his escape in Harry's car. The car is laden with explosives and Harry has activated the fuse. BOOM! The car explodes. Cool Harry shades his eyes from the blast, then says in his inimitable way, "A man's got to know his limitations." Not bad counsel.

To know our own limitations is to avoid two major snares in life: false expectations, which ultimately end in disappointment, and living a fantasy life in a world of make believe. If I lack mathematical aptitude, have poor eyesight, and am in my mid-forties, I should probably stop dreaming about becoming an astronaut.

A most poignant example of how fantasy plays havoc with reality happened while I was observing a civil war reenactment. These are colorful, educational and most enchanting affairs. As the first day came to a close, I was observing the camp of one of the armies. It was like going back in time—the men were playing period games, horses were being tended to, singing was heard around campfires, and the smoke from tent stoves was billowing lazily up through the late autumn sky. My revelry was cut short when two campaigners came trudging along the road. Completely oblivious to my presence, one was lamenting to his friend about how he was neck high in debt. I heard him say that as soon as he returned home he planned to max out his credit cards and then file for bankruptcy. The merchants, who in good faith, had sold him his resplendent uniform, handsome sword, and fine Italian replica Enfield rifle, would never feed their families based on the profits earned from this one who allowed himself to overindulge his fantasies.

> *The blessing of the LORD brings wealth, and he adds no trouble to it* (Prov. 10:22).

44

KEYS TO GREATNESS

People who are considered successful and have reached their potential have certain things in common.

Setting goals is the first key they used to reach their success. Without goals to get us to a predetermined destination, we begin to confuse activity with achievement. This is like being lost while driving and speeding up in hopes of finding our way. We don't find our way, we just get lost in a larger area. Goals help keep us focuses on our target destination.

A second characteristic successful people have is their ability to major in the majors; to grasp the profundity of what Dwight D. Eisenhower said when asked to what he attributed his success to as Supreme Allied Commandeer in Europe during WWII. Eisenhower replied, "I found that the urgent things were seldom important, and that the important things were seldom urgent." The ability to focus on the vital few rather than the trivial many is a distinguishing mark of the high performer.

Another quality that highfliers possess is their judicious selection of friends. Where we go determines whom we meet. Whom we meet determines how we think. How we think determines what we do. And what we do determines our destiny. Quality people avoid those who were born crying, live complaining, and die disappointed. It is easier for one negative thinking person to drag down five positive thinking people than it is for five positive thinking people to raise up one negative thinking person. Along this same line, I once heard a minister say that it was easier to give new birth than to raise the dead!

Dreamers talk much and do little. Achievers talk little and do much. So many people are always getting ready to start something tomorrow that they would make Hamlet look impetuous.

Dream big and work hard so your dreams can stand the test of the daylight.

> *So Jesus called them to him and said, "As you know, the kings and great men of the earth lord it over the people; but among you it is different. Whoever wants to be great among you must be your servant"* (Mark 10:42-44).

45

LOVING PEOPLE AND USING MONEY

A friend of mine related a story to me about when he was seated next to a mutual acquaintance of ours on a coast-to-coast flight. This celebrated, self-promoting mavin was touting her latest self-help book. My friend happened to ask her how many people she thought might read her new book. With sniffing haughtiness she replied that that wasn't the issue, the important thing was how many people would *buy* her book. Having participated in a sales rally with this five foot two inch bundle of kinetic arrogance, I find it quite plausible that this lady loves money and uses people. She doesn't give a hoot whether her books help people or not! Her attitude seems to be, "My objective is to get money out of your pocket and into my bank account!"

Money isn't bad if we use it rather than serve it.

But to think that money is neutral or depersonalized is to run the risk of having the milk of human kindness sucked from our bones. "Giving," Richard Foster says in his book, *The Celebration of Discipline,* "dethrones money." Giving frees us to care. The power of money that seeks to dominate us cannot coexist with benevolence. And who's to say that generosity is not a factor of good health. The late psychiatrist Dr. Karl Menninger said that he could not remember having ever treated a generous person.

Be full of love for others, following the example of Christ who loved you (Ephesians 5:2).

For you have been given freedom: not freedom to do wrong, but freedom to love and serve each other (Galatians 5:13).

46

MEANINGFUL PRODUCTIVITY

In regards to meaningful productivity, it's good to remember that it isn't so much what we know but how we use what we have. Here are some ideas on how to gain the "differential difference" that gives us an edge in the big world of business.

First: Believe in what you do. People are more convinced by the intensity of your beliefs than by the soundness of your reasoning.

Second: Have fun doing what you're doing. The person having fun will always outperform and outlast the person who merely works out of a sense of duty. One has a mission and one has a job. And most people can tell the difference!

Third: Become a "human engineer." This is especially important if you deal with people. Ninety percent of your success will depend on your people skills and only ten percent on your product knowledge.

Fourth: Promise long; deliver short! Most people have this exactly reversed—they over-promise and under-deliver.

Fifth: Stop being part of the problem by complaining or gossiping. We all have three options open to us:

- Keep working to resolve the problem.

- Accept it.

- If the cost of acceptance is too high, leave it. We are not shackled to the wall. When we accept this it eliminates our license to bellyache.

Sixth: Don't strive so hard to be good but strive to be effective. Highly productive people are effective at the 20% of the things that produce 80% of their results.

Seventh: Highly productive people reserve the right to maintain their focus and reduce interruptions. We cannot always oblige others, but we can always speak obligingly.

Eighth: Have a bias for action. We tend to overstudy situations. Do your homework, but then act upon it!

> *Yes, every man is a fool who gets rich on earth but not in heaven* (Luke 12:21).

47

ON LEADERSHIP

Many of us remember Chuck Yeager as the first person to fly faster than the speed of sound. It happened on October 14, 1947 and the plane was the Bell X-1. What many people don't know is that Chuck Yeager was also an outstanding fighter pilot during WWII. Yeager was blessed with exceptional vision. On one occasion, he was leading a fighter group for the first time when he spied a much larger enemy formation up ahead. He called out over his radio to warn his fellow pilots, but because they could not see the enemy for themselves, they disregarded his alarm. As a result, they were badly injured but never doubted Yeager after that incident.

Leadership is not in the title, but in the execution. There are people with high-sounding titles who are not leading but merely taking a walk. And there are those who do not have a title but greatly influence the thoughts and actions of others.

Leaders must have two important qualities that distinguish them from the others: vision and the ability to win the confidence of the people they lead. As with Yeager, these qualities are sometimes not apparent at first to either those who appoint or those intended to follow. A leader might very well experience resistance to their ascendancy. People who lack objectivity or perceive the world to be revolving in a 360% circle around their own navel will surely contest any advancement but their own. Blinded by self-ambition, they cannot discern that they are out of their depth and that the whole process would be better served by lending their efforts to support the most qualified person.

Just how should we describe vision? Vision must have a "faith factor," and a "stretch factor." We must believe and reach before we ever can hope to experience success.

> *He appointed judges throughout the nation in all the larger cities, and instructed them: "Watch your step—I have not appointed you—God has; and he will stand beside you and help you give justice* (2 Chronicles 19:5).

48

SERVICE: THE KEY TO SURVIVAL

We live in a communications and service driven society. The paradox is that so many who count on rendering a service as a livelihood ignore the certainty that they represent the overhead and their customers and clients represent the profit.

Money is the evidence of what kind of service we give. I heard a young person say recently that they wanted to make a lot of money. "The only people who make money work at the mint," my friend the late Earl Nightingale used to say. "The rest of us have to earn it!"

Because of the age of specialization that we find ourselves in today, broad windows of opportunity abound. I know a young couple who are not afraid to get their hands a little dirty. They started a cleaning service four years ago and today make more money than many of the doctors whose offices they clean.

A law of the universe says that if we help others to prosper, then we ourselves will prosper. This law also states that we cannot delude others without being deluded ourselves. Eventually, the practitioners of expediency and duplicity will be attacked by truth in full armor. They may get away with it for a while, but ultimately, it will be shouted from the rooftops.

Businesses having low quality service usually average only a one percent return on sales, and lose, on the average, two percent of market share per year. Businesses with high quality of service average twelve percent return on sales, gain market share at a rate of six percent per year, and charge significantly higher prices.

Customer service is a contact sport, though unlike any other sport, the objective here is to see that the other guy wins. If they win, we win!

Don't be selfish; don't live to make a good impression on others. Be humble, thinking of others as better than yourself (Philippians 2:3).

49

THIN SKINS AND THICK HEARTS

I remember a great line from the old comic strip, Pogo: "We have met the enemy and they is us!" Some people never miss an opportunity to hurt themselves.

I heard a speaker one time say that we are a society of people who have thin skins and thick hearts. I asked him what he meant by the remark. He said that we are too quick to take offense today. With synthetic indignation we rail against supposed wrongs. Being all caught up in the thick of small things can cause us to miss the bigger picture. When we become overly sensitive, we begin to operate based on our feelings, which impairs our ability to objectively deal with the future. We lose our grip on logic and common sense and become casualties in the struggle to maintain emotional equilibrium and sound judgment.

How many careers have been ruined by one bad

day or because of one thoughtless remark? Some people may recall seeing Jimmy the Greek's television career as a sports color commentator unravel faster than a pair of cheap socks, due to an inappropriate racial observation. It swiftly ended the career that had taken the man years to build.

A thin skin leads to a thick heart. When we are overly vigilant about life's slings and arrows coming our way, we develop a lack of sensitivity for others. The fat of indifference envelopes our hearts, and we lose the capacity for empathy, i.e., feeling the other fellow's misery in our own heart.

Our nation has the most generous and spiritual people on earth and also the most wealthy, so we must learn to have a balance between the earthly—buying and selling, and the divine—giving and receiving.

Take My yoke upon you, and learn from Me, for I am gentle and humble in heart; and you shall find rest for you souls (Matt. 11:29).

50

TWO KINDS OF PEOPLE

It strikes me that there are two kinds of people in the workplace today: those who are constantly preoccupied with their rights, privileges, or entitlements, and those who are concerned about their duties.

Those concerned about their rights stand on the curbstones of life and watch the parade of life pass by. When they speak with cynical criticism, they become part of the *problem* rather than part of the *solution*. On the other hand, the people concerned about their duties step into the street and join the army of the committed ones on their way to worthwhile objectives!

Are we part of the solution or part of the problem? Our answer measures our level of maturity. People who are critical are brothers to the saboteur while those promoting harmony and order demonstrate their maturity. Age does not matter, for we have all seen people in their upper years that we know will die terminally silly!

Having interviewed many people over the years, I can say without equivocation that I would rather hire attitude and train skill than hire skill and try to change attitudes! You can pay a person with a bad mental attitude three times as much money and all you'll have is a person with a bad attitude who's three times richer.

Choices, not chance, determine our destiny! The choice to be positive must be made again and again.

What fools the nations are to rage against the Lord! How strange that men should try to outwit God! (Psalm 2:1).

51

HOW TO GET PROMOTED

There were two men working side by side on a loading dock at a large truck terminal. Suddenly, a limousine swung into the yard and stopped close to them. The older of the two men approached the limousine. They carried on a brief conversation, and then the limo sped off.

As the two men resumed their work, the younger man inquired as to who the man was. "Why, that's Mr. Merriweather," the older man replied, "He owns this terminal." "How's it that you know him?" the younger man pressed. The older man said, "Well, twenty years ago he and I worked on this very dock, just like you and me."

After a few minutes the young man said, "If ya don't mind my askin', how's it that he owns this here terminal, and you're still workin' on the dock?" The older man paused reflectively, and then said, "I guess he went to work for the company, and I went to work for seventy-five cents an hour."

Many people don't realize it, but they control their own promotions. A law of the universe says that if we are willing to do more than we are paid to do, eventually we will be paid for more than we actually do! It may not happen immediately, but it must eventually happen for that is an immutable law.

Another way of stating this law is that we may reap from a field different than the one in which we sowed, but we will reap *what* we sow. Some people are too busy keeping score. They begin to expect more pay for doing what is normally required of them. This only serves to disqualify them in the eyes of those who have the power to promote them.

> *If you exalt wisdom, she will exalt you. Hold her fast and she will lead you to great honour* (Prov. 4:8).

52

LEADING OR FOLLOWING?

In the 1940s there was a munitions plant located in a small mid-western town. Almost everyone who lived there worked at the plant. Like so many plants across the country supporting the war effort, they worked around the clock.

A supervisor on the first shift would always walk to work the same way. Every day he would stop at the little jewelry store on Main Street and look in the window at a certain clock. This continued for three years. The shop owner eventually became very curious about this, thinking the man was trying to make up his mind about purchasing the clock. One day the shop owner could stand it no longer and decided to ask him.

That morning he stepped out of his shop, met the man, and told him he had been observing him for three years looking at the clock in the window. The jeweler inquired if the man was intending on purchasing the clock. After apologizing for any concern he may have caused, the man explained that he was a supervisor down at the plant and one of his duties was to sound the noon whistle so all the workers would know when to take their lunch break. So every day on his way to work he would check the time by that clock.

The jeweler shook his head in ironic disbelief. He told the man that he had been setting the clock by the noon whistle for the last three years!

A Spanish proverb says that in the land of the blind, the one-eyed man rules. If we have just a little sight, a little understanding, we have great power!

Look at the Lord's prophets. We know how happy they are now because they stayed true to him, even though they suffered greatly for it (James 5:10).

53

OF CHICKENS AND COWS

There was a tremendous clash between two nineteenth century industrial moguls. George Pullman was an inventor and designer of railroad cars. As rail lines expanded and travel increased, he came up with the brilliant idea of sleeping cars. Steel baron Andrew Carnegie did not miss the enthusiastic response by the public.

Soon their two companies were locked in bitter competition for passengers. Fares plummeted and, before long, both companies found themselves in financial difficulty. Realizing that his company's hemorrhaging could soon be disastrous, Carnegie did an unexpected and most admirable thing. Laying aside his pride, he approached Pullman with the suggestion that they merge their two companies, thus insuring profitability. Pullman, who had no shortage of vanity, asked just what the name of this new company would be. Carnegie replied, "Why, the Pullman Car

Company, of course." And so it was done. Carnegie understood that ten percent of a cow is always better than ninety percent of a chicken. Lesser men would have been ruled by their egos.

"Pride goes before a fall," cautions a wise old proverb. We have all seen opportunities squandered by people with greed who look at cents rather than dollars and settle for a big piece of a very small pie rather than a small piece of a very big pie.

Jealousy and covetousness have also undermined many a company's sales force. Bottom feeders will view new people as a threat and decide there are too many sales people for the amount of business available. In truth, good salespeople create business. Whereas bottom feeders wait for what comes along, surface feeders aggressively seek out new business.

> *And one standing alone can be attacked and defeated, but two can stand back-to-back and conquer* (Ecclesiastes 4:12).

54

Persistence

You have to be good before you can become great, and you have to fail before you can be good. Let's debunk all the high-flown rhetoric about there being no such thing as the word "failure" in the lexicon of the high achiever. Most high achievers will admit to early frustrations.

Thomas Edison experienced a thousand failures before he got his light bulb to work. He simply looked upon failure as experimentation. It's all in how we view our mistakes and problems. An old saying in the sport of judo goes, "You earn your black belt by ten thousand falls." The real tragedy in giving up is to be able to see how close we came to success and to know that had we persisted by renewing our hope one more time, the barriers might have fallen and given us the victory.

Having someone who strongly believes in us, or in

our cause, is a powerful incentive. This was the case with Dr. Norman Vincent Peale. He had taken his manuscript for his best-selling book, *The Power of Positive Thinking* to a dozen publishers, all of whom rejected his work. So discouraged was Dr. Peale that he threw the manuscript in the wastebasket with firm instructions for his wife to leave it there. But so strong was her belief in the rich quality of her husband's work that she retrieved the papers from the wastebasket and carried it to one last publishing house. There they recognized its worth and, as they say, the rest is history. Millions of copies have been sold since it was first published in 1952, and the book has been translated into hundreds of languages.

Perfection is a noble ideal, but it is persistence that contains the seeds of victory.

> *And let us not get tired of doing what is right, for after a while we will reap a harvest of blessing.* (Galatians 6:9).

55

The Danger in Haste

In December of 1939 three light British warships cornered the German battleship Graf Spee in the harbor at Montevideo, Uruguay. Through misinformation put out by the English, the captain of the German battleship, Hans Langsdorf, believed a superior British force was waiting for him once he sailed out of the harbor and reached the open sea.

Uruguay had a law stating that any foreign vessel visiting her port had to leave after 72 hours, and so Captain Langsdorf had no alternative but to weigh anchor and put out to sea. The specter of imminent destruction proved too much for the captain and rather than see his ship destroyed or fall into the hands of the enemy, he decided upon a bold but flawed plan of action. Sailing the Graf Spee just outside the harbor, he ordered all engines stopped, and within view of the British ships, he scuttled her. He and his men rowed to shore in lifeboats and requested asylum.

George Santayana, the Spanish-born American philosopher and novelist, said those who fail to learn from history are destined to repeat it. What can we learn from this historical event, which occurred over sixty years ago? Investigate the circumstances. Captain Langsdorf committed an error by reaching a hasty conclusion in the middle of the matter. How often we tend to prematurely reach a decision.

For in Him we live and move and have our being! (Acts 17:28)

56

THE WONDERFUL MIND OF MAN

The mind is truly a wondrous thing. Someone once said if we could build a computer that could do all the things a human brain can do, it would be two city blocks square by ten stories high. In light of computer chips today it would, no doubt, be somewhat smaller, but with the quantum gains in knowledge, probably not by much.

George Washington Carver was both a botanist and a chemist who discovered 32 uses for the common peanut. Another invention, the gondola elevator so prevalent in hotels today, was suggested by a bellman who overheard engineers expressing their vexation as to how to retrofit a grand old hotel. They wanted to build modern elevators without jeopardizing the hotel's internal structural integrity. "Put the elevators on the outside of the building where people could enjoy viewing the city," he suggested.

The killer of a vibrant creative mind is not dull mindedness but conformity. Some wise person made the observation that we are born unique, but in most cases, we die as copies. Why do people with their own talents and gifts try so hard to emulate someone else? God created us unique, so let's live our lives that way.

An acquaintance of mine was telling me not too long ago that he has a difficult time being a walking billboard for clothing manufactures. When he buys a car he insists the dealer remove their nameplate from the rear trunk lid. He tells them that if the car works and he receives good service, he will return in a year to let them put their name back on his car.

Many of us don't use our minds for very big things. Why? Well, the mind comes as standard equipment. When asked what is wrong with people, the late Nobel Prize winner, Dr. Albert Schweitzer, was silent for a moment and then said, "People simply don't think today." Little has changed.

Don't copy the behavior and customs of this world, but be a new and different person with a fresh newness in all you do and think (Romans 12:2).

57

YOU HAVE NOT BECAUSE YOU ASK NOT

I wish I had a dollar for every salesman I've ever seen who was afraid to ask for an order. Henry Ford wanted to demonstrate this point to his people, so he once bought a DeSoto, made by the Chrysler Corporation. He had them park the car in the circular driveway directly across from the main entrance to Ford Headquarters. After several days, everyone was curious as to whose car it was.

He patiently waited for a large staff meeting and had an aide stand up and ask if anyone knew whose DeSoto it was that was parked out front. Mr. Ford then said that the car belonged to him. "Why," the aide was coached to ask, "would you buy a car made by a competitor?" "Because," Mr. Ford growled, "no one around here asked me to buy a Ford!" He forcefully drove home the point that you have to ask for what you want.

We have not because we ask not. Some people are shy about asking for favors, and many more never ask because they're afraid of the prospects of being turned down. If for no other reason than the saving of time, a definite "no" is better than a lingering "maybe."

If we understand the psychology behind asking, we will ask for more. Most people would rather grant a favor than ask for one. It makes one feel good to grant a favor; and it can also give a sense of power.

> *Ask, and you will be given what you ask for. Seek, and you will find, Knock, and the door will be opened. For everyone who asks, receives. Anyone who seeks, finds. If only you will knock, the door will open unto you* (Matt. 7:7).

58

THE CARPENTER'S STORY

When you speak as often as I do, you're always looking for stories that make a point with impact. The following is such a story. I wish I knew the author's name so I could give him or her credit.

It seems that an old carpenter decided that it was time for him to retire. He was a master craftsman and highly esteemed for his excellent work. He knew he would miss the paycheck and the camaraderie, but he needed to retire and be able to enjoy spending time with his wife and extended family.

The homebuilder, whom he had so faithfully served for so many years, hated to see him go, but he understood.

The contractor prevailed upon his old friend, as a personal favor, to stay on for just one more house. The old man agreed, but it wasn't long before it became evident that his heart was no longer in his work. He resorted to shoddy workmanship, cut corners, and used inferior materials. It was a sad way to end an otherwise stellar career.

When the house was completed and he took off his apron for the last time, the builder appeared for the final home inspection. Forgoing this ritual, and with all the various tradesmen gathered around, the contractor presented the keys to his matchless worker. "This is your house" he said, "my gift to you for your faithfulness."

What a shock! If he had only realized that he was building his own house, how differently he would have built it.

And so it is with us. Think of yourself as a carpenter. Build wisely for you will have to reside in what you build.

Life is a do-it-yourself project. Our life tomorrow will be the result of the attitudes and choices we make today.

> *All those who come and listen and obey me are like a man who builds a house on a strong foundation laid upon the underlying rock* (Luke 6:47).